ATHLETE COOKBOOK

Disclaimer Notice:

Please note the information contained within this document is for educational and entertainment purposes only. All effort has been executed to present accurate, up to date, reliable, complete information. No warranties of any kind are declared or implied. Readers acknowledge that the author is not engaged in the rendering of legal, financial, medical or professional advice. The content within this book has been derived from various sources. Please consult a licensed professional before attempting any techniques outlined in this book.

By reading this document, the reader agrees that under no circumstances is the author responsible for any losses, direct or indirect, that are incurred as a result of the use of the information contained within this document, including, but not limited to, errors, omissions, or inaccuracies.

TABLE OF CONTENTS

Chapter 1 Veganism and Sport

What if you want to do sports while vegan? How realistic is it to be competitive in achieving sports results? What do doctors and nutritionists say about this?

Vegan athletes compete with athletes who eat meat if they eat well.

This applies to a variety of athletic disciplines, including triathlon and even bodybuilding, as a group of Australian researchers led by Professor Dilip Gosh has concluded.

The results of the study were presented to the public in the form of a presentation at the annual Institute of Food Technologists (IFT) Annual Meeting & Expo.

Feeding a vegan athlete means that to achieve record sporting results, he or she needs to add products to his or her diet that compensate for the deficiency of other athletes' meat and other animal products.

The impetus for the study was the recent discovery of a burial site for Roman gladiators, which gives good reason to believe that these fierce and indefatigable warriors were vegetarians.

Scientists have also taken into account that some record-breaking athletes, such as Bart Yasso and Scott Jurek, or the triathlete Brendan Brazier, are still vegetarians today.

Official positions of medical and nutritional organizations regarding vegetarianism and veganism

Swiss Health Authority*

"Sufficient intake of vegan vitamin B12 can only be obtained from special additives, but all other nutrients, including calcium and iron, can be obtained from plant products."

The American Dietetic Association*

"Properly designed vegetarian diets, including vegan diets, are healthy and complete, suitable for people of all ages, pregnant and nurturing women, children, teenagers, athletes, and can also help prevent and treat certain diseases" [Position of the American Dietetic Association: vegetarian diets.]

British Food Foundation*

"A balanced vegetarian or vegan diet can be complete, but more extreme diets, such as eating raw materials, are often ineffective and do not provide the full range of essential micronutrients, making them completely unacceptable for children. ...Studies of vegetarian and vegan children in the UK have shown that they develop and grow within normal limits" [Briefing Paper on Vegetarian nutrition]

"Nutritionists of Canada"*

"A properly planned vegetarian diet is healthy, nutritionally complete and can play a positive role in the prevention and treatment of certain diseases" Position of the American Dietetic Association and Dietitians of Canada: Vegetarian diets.

* [www.ncbi.nlm.nih.gov/pubmed/19562864]

* [www.nutrition.org.uk/attachments/106_Vegetarian%20nutrition.pdf]

* [www.eatrightpro.org/-/media/eatrightpro-files/practice/position-and-practice-papers/position-papers/vegetarian-diet.pdf]

* [www.andeal.org/vault/2440/web/JADA_VEG.pdf]

* [EEK_vegan_report_final.docx.pdf]

* [https://my.clevelandclinic.org/health/articles/17593-vegetarianism--heart-health]

* [https://www.hsph.harvard.edu/news/hsph-in-the-news/vegan-diet-health-environment/]

* [www.nhs.uk/live-well/eat-well/the-vegan-diet/]

Dr. Dilip Gosh concluded

According to the results of the research, it is not so important to have a "vegetarian" or "meat-eater" because, in terms of sports nutrition and training outcomes, there is only one thing that counts: sufficient consumption and absorption of several essential nutrients.

Dr. Dilip Gosh has calculated the ideal nutritional formula for athletes who can be either vegan or vegetarian or meat logged: 45-65% of food should be carbohydrates, 20-25% fat, and 10-35% protein (figures may vary depending on training and other factors).

Gosh said that "athletes can achieve full nutrition even on a pure vegetable diet if they are vegan - Vegetarian - if they keep to their calories and regularly consume several essential foods. Gauche cited non-animal sources of iron, creatine, zinc, vitamin B12, vitamin D, and calcium is vital.

One of the most critical success factors for athletes is sufficient iron consumption, says Dr. Dilip Gosh. He stressed that this problem is more acute for female athletes, as this group of vegan athletes, according to his observations, may have a non-anemic iron deficiency. Iron deficiency is primarily affecting the reduction of endurance training results.

Vegans generally characterized by reduced levels of creatine in their muscles, gosh notes, so these athletes must take the issue of their nutritional status very seriously.

Speaking of specific products for athletes, Dr. Dilip Gosh considers the most useful:

-Soy drinks;

-Nuts;

-Orange and yellow vegetables, as well as leafy vegetables (cabbage, herbs);

-Fruit;

-Vitaminized cereal flakes for breakfast;

-Milk and dairy products (for those athletes who consume milk).

Dr. Dilip Gosh noted that his research is very young and that it will take years of scientific observation for athletes to get a detailed picture of the sports training under vegetarian, vegan conditions. However, in his opinion, the forecast for vegan athletes is very favorable.

Athletes who adhere to vegetarian or vegan diets have proven many times that plant food is no worse than an animal to achieve sporting achievements. However, novice athletes often lack some nutrients. We find out how to eat plant foods during intensive sports activities.

Vegan athletes often face particular challenges in meeting their nutrient needs, but with careful dietary planning, this can be avoided. If you need proof, look at Scott Gordon Jurek, an ultra marathonist who trains up to eight hours a day and eats only plant foods. Or the famous boxer Mike Tyson, the great athlete Carl Lewis, tennis player Serena Williams. The list of vegan athletes and vegetarians is extensive.

A vegetarian or vegan diet can fit perfectly into an athlete's training plan. Vegetarian diets usually contain a large amount of "good" carbohydrates - the primary fuel for athletes, without which they can feel sluggish, tired, have problems with kidneys and other organs. Vegetables, fruits, whole grains, nuts, and seeds contain quality carbohydrates, vitamins, minerals, and fiber.

The myth that vegans and vegetarians do not eat protein has been dispelled many times. Vegetable protein sources have low levels of saturated fat and do not contain cholesterol, maintaining a healthy cardiovascular system, unlike animal products. Good protein sources for vegan athletes include quinoa, buckwheat, brown rice, protein-enriched pasta, nuts, tofu, soya milk, soya cheese and yogurt, peanut butter, beans, and peas.

Are there enough plant foods?
However, athletes have some specific issues to consider when planning and following a diet. They should carefully control the intake of vitamin B12, which can be obtained through fortified yeast (not to be confused with bakery products) or through natural additives. In addition to B12, vegan athletes (especially beginners) often face deficiencies in calcium, iron, zinc, iodine, magnesium, vitamin D and riboflavin.

Vegan and vegetarian diets also tend to contain large amounts of fiber, which can lead to meteorism and abdominal bloating if high-fiber foods are consumed immediately before or during exercise. Therefore, these foods are better eaten at least an hour and a half to two hours before a workout, separately from the main meals.

To avoid meteoric influences and to gain strength before exercise, vegan athletes choose alternatives to animal proteins, such as soybean meat, tofu, vegan sausages, and other plant foods.

However, the composition of such products should be carefully read to avoid the harmful additives that are often used in the preparation of vegan protein dishes.

Nutrient requirements can be met with natural plant-based nutritional supplements.

Fortunately, nowadays there are more and more of them! But any additive must be carefully studied because it is often added with gelatin or creatine (which is found in the muscles of animals). In addition to vitamins and minerals, there is also a large amount of plant protein available on the plant products market, which professional athletes can include in their diet.

What products do we recommend?

Athletes or fitness enthusiasts should plan their menus even more carefully than vegans who do not do sports. Include products in your diet that will help you to achieve your sporting goals.

Calcium: tofu, soy, rice and almond drinks, broccoli, cabbage kale, herbs, almonds, tahini, black molasses.

Iron: legumes, nuts, and seeds, wholemeal bread, cereals, root vegetables, dried fruits.

Zinc: legumes, nuts, and seeds, soy products, cereals.

Iodine: seaweed, seaweed, seaweed, apples, oranges, persimmon, spinach.

Magnesium: beans, nuts, and seeds, seaweed, oatmeal, buckwheat, millet, barley groats.

Vitamin D: vitamin-enriched products, sun-dried mushrooms, parsley, vegetable oils.

Vitamin B12: food yeast, soybean products, vitamin-enriched products.

Riboflavin (vitamin B2): whole grains, wholemeal bread, and cereals, tofu, nuts, seeds, bananas, asparagus, figs, avocado.

Chapter 2 Golden rules for vegan athletes

We fix the learned material and adopt these simple but essential rules for vegan athletes.

1. Balance your diet

You don't have to eat only fruits and vegetables or buckwheat and rice. No matter what type of food you choose (vegan or vegetarian), you need to diversify and balance it as much as possible. Remember the nutrients, take vitamin-mineral supplements. Take a blood test at least once every six months to monitor your condition.

2. Consider a week-long meal plan

A pre-defined menu will help you to balance your diet carefully and clearly, and to stick to it with peace of mind. Describe the main meals, snacks, and supplements. If you're starting your vegan-sports journey, this will help you understand what and how much you need to eat. You won't need a nutrition plan anymore in the future, as you'll already know intuitively how to eat correctly.

3. Use the right protein

Take it, as a rule, to consume good protein after training. You can use vegetable protein shakes, which only need to fill with water, or you can make your own by blending soya milk, germinated beans, and banana in a blender. Quickly, deliciously, usefully! And most importantly - no lack of protein.

4. Eat more "good" carbs

If you've given up industrial sugar, chips, cookies, sweets, and other "simple" carbohydrates, it allows you to eat "better"! You can afford to eat some carbohydrates such as buckwheat, brown rice, vegetables, fruits, seeds, and nuts, even in the evening.

Based on the results of several scientific studies, physicians make such objective scientific conclusions:
- A well-balanced vegetarian or vegan diet can support the athlete's performance (ideal for fitness and athletics).

- Provided that protein intake is sufficient to meet the need for nitrogen and essential amino acids (which, as we know, are found in many vegan products), as well as vegetable (which is a reasonably wide range of products - see at the end of the material) and animal (which found in milk and dairy products) proteins - this is an adequate diet for the athlete even during the competition;

- Vegetarians, especially women, are at high risk for anemia, an iron deficiency that can limit an athlete's productivity and stamina, and undermine health in general - and this must be taken into account. But iron deficiency and fatigue are not "purely vegetarian problems"! Endurance problems can also occur in meat-eating athletes - for example, tennis player Venus Williams individually switched to veganism - and Serena Williams has "taken the company" - to cope with the problem of fatigue!

- Vegetarians and vegans have a lower average concentration of creatine in their muscles than meat-eaters, and this can affect performance under extreme strain. If you are serious, it is advisable to take creatine in a sports supplement, and it is 100% vegan.

Scientifically proven that taking creatine in people who do not consume meat leads to significant increases in athletic performance, as well as improved brain function.

Interestingly, the increase in the results after including creatine in the diet is more significant in vegan athletes than meat-eating athletes show!

-Creatine stored in the muscles. Our body, mainly the liver and kidneys, can produce creatine, but only about 1 gram per day. Another 1 gram per day can be absorbed from food. Such a ratio, 1:1 1 gram mastered, 1 gram produced is optimal and necessary for athletes. Unfortunately, "in nature" creatine is found only in meat products. But this issue is easily solved for vegans and vegetarians with the help of a sports additive.

- Many athletes use the transition to a vegetarian diet as a way to reduce weight, which can be necessary for runners, boxers, and other athletes. But it is important to note that excessive weight loss does not always improve results. Therefore, athletes, or instead of their coach and doctor, should monitor weight loss when switching to veganism. If you lose a healthy weight rapidly, it can't be right, and you need to review your diet with a calculator in your hand.

Fortunately, there are no problems with ethical, vegetable protein sources in both vegan and raw diets Thus, on a purely vegetable menu, it is possible to do sports, fitness, and to lead an active lifestyle without any restrictions or problems.

Practical tips for Vegan

Vegans don't eat meat, so where do you get vitamin B12?

Yes, it's a problem for an athlete; it's almost impossible to eat B12 on a vegetable diet in the right amount. Even more fundamental is the question for women who lose blood during the monthly cycle. The only simple solution is to take a vegan food supplement containing vitamin B12.

How can I meet my body's protein needs?

After training, you need to consume enough protein. The main rule of recovery after any workout is to consume enough protein. Ovo-lacto-vegetarians can afford eggs or yogurt.

Vegans will have to settle for vegetable protein - but it's not "worse," and there are a lot of protein sources!

Vegan sources of protein:
-Hemp seed or flour;
-Grain legumes;
-Soybean protein powder - sports additive
-Tofu;
-Beans;
-Unsweetened soy milk.

Constant hunger, especially during training days!

Consume protein. Lack of protein in your diet can lead to sudden insulin jumps and falls. If you are active, fit, you need more protein than sedentary people. Consume plenty of proteins and carbohydrates in each meal: together, they will be absorbed evenly, and you will avoid sudden changes in energy and lethargy that can exhaust you and prevent you from training to the fullest. Avoid trans fats, and do not neglect quality fats.

With an active lifestyle, it's categorically not helpful.

Vegan sources of healthy fat:

Extra virgin olive oil;

Fruits of avocado;

Roasted seeds and nuts.

Linseed oil;

Hemp oil.

Tense muscles

Pay attention to sufficient sodium and calcium intake, especially if you are sweating heavily during training. Consume sodium and food and salt in the diet.
Good vegan sources of calcium:
Almond nuts;
Beans;
Spinach, cabbage, and other dark green leafy vegetables;
Sesame seed;
Sunflower seed.

Fast fatigue, lethargy, difficult to train

Take a blood test to make sure you are not at risk for anemia. Iron comes out with then, like sodium and calcium. The more intense your training, the more iron you need, and this is a problem, especially for runners.

Vegan products rich in iron:
Iron-enriched breakfasts, oatmeal;
Dried peas;
Bran;
Peanut butter;
Apricots;
Green beans;
Treacle;
Soybeans;
Plum juice;
Pea soup;
Raisins;

Any fruit juice enriched with iron;
Walnut, cashew, pecan nut, almond nut.
Eat full and healthy food, and achieve excellent results!

A vegan bodybuilder's diet is a lifestyle.

To begin with, the concept of nutrition for a vegan bodybuilder does not only include sufficient protein intake, calorie control, and fat dosing. It is a system in which success depends on everything: the frequency of meals, the total amount of protein and bio-additives taken, the amount of liquid consumed, the combination of foods, and many other factors.

How rationally a bodybuilder can organize his or her meals - from the number of meals to the amount of water he or she drinks - depends directly on the result. Success, in this case, is a derivative of the sophisticated approach, not just the influence of protein.

Protein can be obtained from both animal and plant foods. Also, proteins derived from plant foods are digested much more easily by the human body. Consumption of protein from plant foods - does not provoke an increase in cholesterol levels, high blood pressure, and the development of cardiovascular disease.

Vegetable protein is quite suitable as a building material of cells; besides, it delivers in an organism the equal quantity of amino acids. Protein is contained in legumes, nuts, cereals, hemp, seeds, rice, fruits, and vegetables.

Especially many essential amino acids, which contribute to muscle mass, are found in hemp proteins. Hemp is essentially a unique plant: two-thirds of the protein in cannabis is edestin, a protein very similar in composition to that found in human blood. This protein is straightforward to set up and is a real find for vegan bodybuilders.

Yellow peas, brown rice, and soybean are also excellent sources of protein, but you should not overdo it. There should be only moderate amounts of protein, even healthy protein, as excessive consumption can cause an elementary allergy.

Shredded food helps keep fit. Many of our own experience advises to eat 6-10 times a day, but in small Servings: With this approach, the muscles will continuously receive the necessary components, so it will be much easier to build muscle. Not to feel hunger and at the same time not to overeat - here is the golden mean to which any bodybuilder aspires, and bodybuilder-vegan and supposes.

Of course, frequent consumption of food causes some difficulties, because it is impossible to be always at the refrigerator or stove. Athletes find a way out of this situation: they still have food with them, but most importantly - they plan their meal! Vegan bodybuilders can't afford to eat on vegetables - what they have to eat. Every morning they make up their daily diet and take the necessary food with them.

In many cases, it makes sense to use a ready-made food set, consisting of many products that are healthy and delicious at the same time. It can be peas, rice, hemp, flax, and other products that include a balanced amount of amino acids.

Nuts, sunflower seeds, and other blanks can be used from the usual pre-prepared products - small stocks that take up little space and are very useful at the right time. It is advisable to avoid perishable foods. For example, if boiled rice or potatoes placed in a particular food container, they will not spoil and will become a reliable support for the bodybuilder in between workouts.

Useful tips for vegan athletes:

- Forget about artificially over-treated food and gradually switch to natural food: only in such food, the body will be able to draw strength and energy for itself.

- Give up fried food in favor of boiled food - this will help your body and your muscles.

- If during training or at night you notice cramps in your legs, it means that you are short of sodium and potassium. Try to increase the intake of these elements into the body - for example, food supplements will help.
- If you're worried about sleeping problems, add zinc and magnesium to your diet to help your body relax after exhausting workouts.
- Eat fruit for breakfast - it will not only nourish your body with nutrients but will also wake it up, stimulating it to take action. And the right start of the day for an athlete is the key to a successful day!

- Let your diet contain at least one Servings: of green salad per day - the amino acids it contains will be great for muscle growth.

Chapter 3 Whole foods are the basis of the vegan bodybuilder's diet

To cope with the load and achieve results, a vegan bodybuilder should emphasize whole foods. Fruits, vegetables, nuts, cereals, legumes, seeds are probably the healthiest and the best food that can provide the body with everything it needs. Of course, you need to diversify your diet. You can always choose from a variety of products that are both separately and in combination will be the basis for a full exercise.

Even though the products have almost everything you need, it is not always possible, due to various circumstances, to get a balanced set of vitamins, minerals, and trace elements from natural products.

It makes sense to include nutritional supplements containing proteins, carbohydrates, fats, and amino acids.

What kind of food additives shown to bodybuilders? Naturally, multivitamins, glucose, vitamin B-12, calcium, iron, vitamins E, and C. Do not abuse vitamins - one dose a day will be enough. In general, forming your style of diet, you should proceed from the formula optimal for bodybuilders: 40% protein, 30% fat, and 30% carbohydrates.

HEALTHY
Food

Weightlifting on a vegan diet: what does science say?

Many weightlifters think that a vegan diet can have a detrimental effect on their performance because of the lower protein content of a typical vegan diet. Other weightlifters believe that a vegan diet improves its training regimen, reducing fatigue, and improving overall health. Unfortunately, there are no direct studies of weightlifting vegans, but there are enough studies that can be extrapolated to vegans.

When reading this book, keep in mind that weightlifting can be divided into two types:
Bodybuilding - to achieve the most visible muscles.
Powerlifting - to produce the most power.

Energy

Carbohydrates, fats, proteins, and alcohol are sources of energy. Burdening exercises, exercises in which muscles push or pull any weight, are used to develop and maintain muscle strength and require more power than people who lead a sedentary lifestyle. The amount of this energy varies depending on the training regimen as well as other factors, including levels of exercise, gender, non-training habits, and genetics. Because of the different needs, there is no single simple formula for calculating calorie intake, and it is the subject of experimentation.
It is important to note that eating insufficient calories to meet calorie requirements will lead to a reduction in muscle mass. Consumption of sufficient calories saves muscle protein, which would otherwise be used to produce energy. Attention to hunger can be a good guideline for understanding whether you are getting enough energy.

For an overall rough estimate, novice weightlifters have increased muscle mass and volume. And reduced-fat deposits on a diet containing about 18 kilocalories per pound of the body per day -3,240 kilocalories per day for a 180-pound person. [39.68 kilocalories per kg per day; 3240 kilocalories per day for a person weighing 180-pound or 81.65 kg]. In another study, highly trained male bodybuilders ate 22.7 kilocalories/lb. (4068 kilocalories/day for a 180-pound person) [50.04 kilocalories/kg; 4068 kilocalories/day for an 179-pound or 81.65-kg person].

Protein

Depending on the source, protein requirements for weightlifters range from unbiased recommendations for a nutritious diet (RDA) to values that are four times higher than those recommendations. But early 20th-century work showed that exercises do not change protein demand, and, until the 1970s, this statement accepted without further research. More recently, additional protein demand studies have carried out on athletes, and their interpretations have differed.

Determining how much protein a person needs is often done by using the results of the nitrogen balance study. Nitrogen is a component of amino acids, the bricks that make up protein, and it can serve as a marker of protein metabolism. Positive nitrogen balance means that a person takes more nitrogen than he or she exudes, and therefore uses it to build muscles. Negative nitrogen balance means that nitrogen is released more than it consumed, which means that muscle tissue destroyed. Nitrogen balance is an inaccurate method of measuring protein demand; what matters is whether a person's muscle mass, strength, or speed increased.

Let's consider the two most relevant studies. In the first one, Tarnopolsky MA studied 12 men who started an intensive training program with a weight of 1.5 hours a day, six days a week. They compared the month in which the subjects received a carbohydrate supplement (on a diet that takes into account the production of 1.4 g/kg protein per day) to the month in which the athletes were given an increased amount of protein (a total of 2.6 g/kg protein per day). They found that an increase in protein intake of 1.6 g/kg to 1.7 g/kg was necessary to achieve nitrogen balance. However, muscle size and strength increased equally in both modes.

The authors believed that additional amino acids for muscle buildup during carbohydrate increase came from amino acid reserves in the gastrointestinal tract, kidneys, or liver. These sources are small and will eventually be exhausted.

The second study was conducted by Lemon PW and co-authors on six latus vegetarian bodybuilders [latus vegetarian vegetarians eating eggs and dairy products] who had been intensively practicing for at least 3 years.2 Culturists usually ate 2.77 g/kg protein each. After they reduced their intake of protein to 1.05 g/kg, the group remained in a nitrogen balance, and no loss of body weight (nonfat) occurred. However, two people found a negative nitrogen balance when eating 1.05 g/kg of protein. These results showed that the required amount of protein for most advanced bodybuilders is close to 1.05 g/kg, but that some people may have higher requirements.

Taken together, these studies, conducted on a small number of athletes, suggest that protein requirements (per body weight unit) may be higher in the early stages of exercise (when muscles increase, and protein is maintained) than when muscle growth stops.

The Food and Nutrition Council, which sets up the RDA, has reviewed the Lemon PW study and co-authors and other studies and concluded that there is not enough evidence to show that weighted training increases RDA protein above 0.8 g/kg for healthy adults.

Some vegan health experts recommend slightly higher levels of protein intake (0.9-1.0 g/kg body weight) than RDA for vegans at all. The Food and Nutrition Council recently stated that if complementary sources of protein (usually a blend of beans and cereals during the day) used, the protein requirements of vegetarians are not higher than those of non-vegetarians.

It should be noted that the RDA for protein takes into account the safety factor, so that many people who are sedentary, following the RDA, will get more protein than they need. Taking into account the information discussed above, as well as the lack of other specific studies, it seems reasonable to conclude that the protein requirement for most vegetarians is between about 0.8 and 1.5 g/kg (0.36 and 0.68 g/lb.) of body weight.

The most extensive study of vegans to date shows that they consume about 0.9 g of protein per kilogram of body weight and receive 13% of their energy from protein.

Thus, if vegan eats 18 kcal/lb., which appears to be the lower limit of severe weightlifters, he or she will consume 1.3 g of protein/kg of body weight spontaneously, most likely satisfying his or her protein needs. However, if the increase in calorie intake is mainly due to more carbohydrates, such as pasta, the percentage of protein may be lower.

For this reason, weightlifting vegans should also try to choose foods with high protein content. Legumes, soybean products, wheat gluten (seitan) are the typical vegan food with the most top protein content. Vegans can also take protein supplements, although this is not necessary. If vegans occasionally take supplements, Naturade produces several vegan protein supplements, including a soybean-free protein supplement for people with soy allergies or who do not want to include additional soya in their diet. Most health food stores can order these supplements if they are not available.

Fat

Based on the study of athletes in long-term physical activity sports, some researchers believe that fat is an essential part of an athlete's diet. Dietary foods that are too low in fat (15% or less in fat) can weaken immunity, reduce intramuscular fat reserves (which can save muscle protein), and reduce overall energy consumption. Consumption of more fat can also reduce the likelihood of menstrual irregularities in women compared to a low-fat diet.

The average amount of vegan fat consumed is about 28% of total calories. Some weightlifters try to avoid fat in the diet to get rid of subcutaneous fat. But this is not recommended for vegans whose food already contains relatively small amounts of fat. A reasonable estimate of the best measure of fat in a heavyweight vegan diet is about 20 to 28 percent of the total calories.

Fried foods and hydrogenated oils (such as those found in many kinds of margarine) should not be used to increase fat consumption. They have an increased content of trans-fatty acids, which increases the risk of heart disease. It is better to choose avocado, nuts, flax seeds, olive oil, rape oil, tofu, and chocolate.

All vegans should pay attention to the consumption of omega-3 fatty acids. As well as essential amino acids, omega-3 helps to carry out nerve impulses; form membranes around the brain, heart, muscles, and other organs; and maintain optimal conditions for the health of the heart and vessels.

These needs can usually meet by taking one teaspoon of linseed oil per day. Pushed flaxseed, rape oil, and walnuts are also good sources of omega-3 fatty acids.

Carbohydrates

Carbohydrates are the primary fuel used in weightlifting exercises, and some researchers suggest using 6 g of carbs per kilogram of body weight (2.7 g/lb.) per day, or about 55 to 60 percent of the total calorie intake. Those weightlifting vegans who follow the recommendations for total calorie intake and the protein and fat intake recommendations above will automatically meet their carbohydrate needs.

Vitamins and minerals

When the amount of food consumed increases, as is the case with weightlifters, the use of vitamins and minerals will also naturally increase. Weightlifters have not been studying the intake of more vitamins and minerals than RDA. Weightlifter vegans should pay attention to the typical nutrients recommended for all vegans (mainly vitamin B12, vitamin D, and calcium). Still, there is no reason to believe that any of these nutrients needed in more quantities than those contained in a typical diversified vegan diet.

Female bodybuilders, especially those with amenorrhea (cessation of menstruation), should pay particular attention to obtaining sufficient calcium and vitamin D. RDA for adults is 1000 mg for calcium and five μg (200 IU) for vitamin D. Some physicians recommend, taking multivitamin supplements containing 50 to 100% RDA for all.

Drying stage

For bodybuilders, increasing muscle mass is only half the battle. The second half is the reduction of the fat layer so that the muscles can be seen better. Powerlifters can also try to lose fat for the competition to get into the lighter weight category.

Vegan diets are generally less caloric, and vegans typically have a lower Body Mass Index (a weight estimate based on height differences).

Vegans tend to have a lower percentage of body fat, but these figures are not always statistically significant.

Bodybuilders are often called upon to "eat all the time" or to eat about six smaller meals instead of three larger ones.

In addition to providing continuous energy for exercise, recent studies have shown that this can certainly be an effective way of reducing body fat. In a unique study, researchers at the University of Georgia have studied 62 elite athletes and their energy consumption by hours. Among the athletes were rhythmic gymnasts, rhythmic gymnasts, middle- and long-distance runners. Food and energy measurements were made on an hourly basis on a regular training day. A connection of at least 300 kcal deficit (when at least 300 kcal of energy per day was burned more than eaten) with large fat deposits was established. Scientists have suggested that energy deficiency provokes a slowdown in metabolism so that fat can be deposited in spite of high energy consumption. They noted that it is counterproductive to reduce energy consumption below the required level to lose weight.

Although the study not conducted on bodybuilders, the results could directly be applied to them. Given that bodybuilders have been "snacking" for years, it seems reasonable to conclude that eating multiple times a day to equalize the amount of energy consumed and consumed should help bodybuilders reduce body fat.

Creatine

Creatine (also known as creatine monohydrate) is the only food additive that consistently demonstrates improved strength and muscle mass. The main advantage of creatine is that it reduces fatigue during repeated series of intense exercise, and therefore it allows you to train more. Although there are still questions to be answered, we are continually getting more convincing opinions about creatine.

Creatine is a component of PCR and can be synthesized in the human body. It also comes with food: meat and fish. PCR provides energy during short bursts of intense exercise such as weightlifting and sprinting or during much high-intensity training such as football, rugby, and hockey. The depletion of PCR reserves in muscles is associated with fatigue during such exercises. The additional use of creatine has shown an increase in performance in these sports, especially in people whose muscle creatine levels have initially been at the lower end of the norm.

Vegetarians have lower levels of creatine in their blood, urine, and red blood cells. This does not necessarily mean that they have lower levels of creatine in their muscles, where it most needed during exercise.

In one study, vegetarians and meat-eaters took 7 g of creatine three times a day for six days. The strength developed by vegetarians after three approaches of exercise increased significantly after six days of supplementation, while meat-eaters did not change. In another study of vegetarians, creatine supplementation did not improve their strength levels.

Typically, a daily intake of 20-30 g of creatine, broken down into smaller doses over a day lasting five to six days, showed an increase in performance. Taking such a dose of creatine for more than six days is not an advantage, and after the initial "loading" phase, taking 2 g per day maintains creatine levels for at least one month. To increase the effect, some researchers suggest taking creatine at monthly intervals.

The "loading" stage for vegetarians and non-vegetarians is likely to be identical, as the intake of creatine with food from non-vegetarians is negligibly small compared to the dose of creatine taken with the supplement. However, since the average meat-eater consumes 1-2 g of creatine per day, 30% of which destroyed during cooking, it may be necessary to increase the amount of creatine added to vegetarians to 3-4 g per day during the maintenance phase.

Powdered creatine with a sugar solution, such as a sports drink or fruit juice, increases the speed with which muscles suck up creatine.

Safety of creatine intake

In the short term, the creatine administration does not show problems in people without kidney disease. In one study, liver and kidney function markers were observed after five days of 20 g/day use, and no issues were found. Similar studies confirmed these results. No noticeable changes were seen in people who had been on 20 g/day for up to 5 weeks. However, there are some episodic (unaccounted for) reports of muscle cramps and tears caused by creatine use.

The long-term effects of creatine use have not been studied, but there have been no reports of long-term problems so far. British weightlifters have been using creatine for three to five years without any issues.

There is one case of a person with kidney disease whose kidney function worsened after taking creatine. Therefore, people with kidney disease warned against taking creatine.

Chapter 4 Vegan cuisine, breakfast recipes

1. Buckwheat breakfast

Cook time: 1 Hour 20 Minutes
Servings: 4

ENERGY VALUE PER SERVING:
Calories: 281kcal
Protein: 6.1 grams
Total Fat: 11.2 grams
Carbohydrates: 41.6 grams

INGREDIENTS:
1 cup Buckwheat grits
Chopped parsley to taste
Chopped coriander
Celery stem chopped to taste
½ Lemon
2 tablespoons Olive oil
Soy sauce to taste

COOKING INSTRUCTION:
- Wash buckwheat, pour 2 glasses of boiling water, salt, cover with the lid, and cover with a towel. After 45-60 minutes, buckwheat can be eaten without losing any nutritional value. It is better to do it at night.
- Steamed the buckwheat in a heated plate and season with olive oil, soy sauce, lemon juice or chopped lemon and shredded herbs, mix.
- Serve with sliced vegetables such as sweet pepper, carrots, pumpkin, radish, and green cocktail.

2. Crispy Hash- Browns

Cook time: 20 Minutes
Servings: 4

ENERGY VALUE PER SERVING:
Calories: 229kcal
Protein: 2.4 grams
Total Fat: 15.4 grams
Carbohydrates: 22.6 grams

INGREDIENTS:
3 tablespoons Olive oil
500 g Potatoes
Salt to taste
Black pepper ground to taste

COOKING INSTRUCTION:
- Peel potatoes and rub on a large grater. Put in the colander and squeeze out the excess moisture. In the meantime, heat the olive oil in a pan over medium heat, but do not let it smoke.
- Place the potatoes in a frying pan and flatten with a fork in a thin layer: salt and pepper. Give a few minutes to brown and turn the pancake upside down with a large spatula. Fry until crispy.

TIP TO THE RECIPE:
It's a recipe for a classic Hash-Browns. You can add garlic, onions, and different herbs if you like.

3. A snack of chickpeas, olives, and red onions

Cook time: 50 Minutes
Servings:4

ENERGY VALUE PER SERVING:
Calories: 171 Kcal
Protein: 7.5 grams
Total Fat: 4.8 grams
Carbohydrates: 23.3 grams

INGREDIENTS:
430 g Canned chickpea
2 tablespoons Olives without pips
1 Red onion
1 tablespoon Chopped parsley
½ Lemon
Salt to taste
Freshly ground black pepper to taste
Olive oil to taste

COOKING INSTRUCTION:
- In a small bowl, mix chickpea, finely sliced olives, finely sliced red onions, parsley, juice, and half a lemon peel.

- Pour salt and pepper. Slightly remember the mass with a fork or a jerk (the mash should not look like mashed potatoes, but should be easily molded together).
- Add a lot of olive oil, mix well, and serve.

TIP TO THE RECIPE:

This appetizer is a great sandwich dish to serve. For this purpose, spread a little tahini on one toast, then lay out a couple of slices of red bell peppers and chickpea mass. Cover with the second toast and press lightly. Cut in half and serve.

4. Coconut manna with strawberry

Cook time: 15 Minutes
Servings: 1

ENERGY VALUE PER SERVING:
Calories: 791kcal
Protein: 15 grams
Total Fat: 55.2 grams
Carbohydrates: 87.1 grams

INGREDIENTS:
80g Manna grits
50 ml Coconut cream
250 ml Coconut milk
1 tablespoon Sugar
1 pcs Vanilla pod
1 tablespoon Fried coconut chips
20 g Strawberries

COOKING INSTRUCTION:
- Cut the vanilla pod into two parts in the middle. Scrape the black vanilla seeds out of the pod with the sharp surface of the knife - the more seeds, the more aromatic the porridge will be. Postpone it.
- Peel the strawberries cut them into four pieces. Put it aside.

- Combine coconut milk and cream in a saucepan; add the vanilla seeds and the pod itself. Add sugar, put it on medium heat and bring it to the boil. Remove from the fire and allow to stand under the lid for a few minutes. Return to medium heat and gently spray the semolina. Cook until thick, continually stirring to prevent lumps from forming. When the cereal thickens, please remove it from the fire and intervene with the coconut chips. Gently remove the vanilla pod, rinse, dry, and retain for future use.
- Serve the porridge with fresh strawberries.

5. Spicy semolina with saffron and cashew

Cook time: 15 Minutes
Servings: 1

ENERGY VALUE PER SERVING:
Calories: 755kcal
Protein: 13.2 grams
Total Fat: 42.6 grams
Carbohydrates: 83.5 grams

INGREDIENTS:
80g Cream of Wheat
1 tablespoon Sugar
280 ml Coconut milk
¼ of a teaspoon ground cinnamon
0.1 teaspoons ground cardamom
Cashew fried to taste
Saffron pinch

COOKING INSTRUCTION:

- Pour coconut milk into the pot. Add ground cardamom, ground cinnamon, and sugar. Place on medium heat and heat to a boil. Remove from the fire and let stand under the lid for 5 minutes. Then strain the milk and return it to the fire.
- Add a pinch of saffron to the milk. Gradually sprinkle the semolina into the hot milk, stirring. Cook over high heat for about 5 minutes until it thickens. Mix the cereal vigorously so that it does not burn and form lumps.
- Remove the porridge from the fire. Decorate with cashews of nuts and serve.

6. Coconut oatmeal with Green Tea Matcha and almonds

Cook time: 15 Minutes
Servings: 2

ENERGY VALUE PER SERVING:
Calories: 801 kcal
Protein: 14.2 grams
Total Fat: 54.9 grams
Carbohydrates: 62 grams

INGREDIENTS:
120g Oatmeal
2.5 tablespoons Sugar
600 ml Coconut milk
4 teaspoon sweet coconut chips
1 teaspoon Green tea (powder)
Almonds taste good

COOKING INSTRUCTION:
- Combine coconut milk and sugar in a pot. Place on medium heat and bring to a boil.
- Sprinkle the oatmeal and cook, stirring for about 5-7 minutes until it thickens.
- Remove from the fire and intervene 1.5-2 teaspoons of green tea powder Matcha.

- Vary the number of green tea Matcha according to the color you want to get: the more (2 teaspoons), the brighter the color and smell of green tea. Less (1 teaspoon) - the color is more pasteli and, therefore, more neutral.)
- Interchange 2 teaspoons of coconut chips, mix well, cover with the lid and let stand for a couple of minutes.
- Serve the porridge with almonds and the remaining coconut chips.

7. Tofu cheese on rice flour

Cook time: 20 Minutes
Servings: 2

ENERGY VALUE PER SERVING:
Calories: 189kcal
Protein: 10.1 grams
Total Fat: 4.3 grams
Carbohydrates: 28.4 grams

INGREDIENTS:
200g Solid tofu
1 Bananas
15½tablespoons Rice flour
A pinch of salt
Sugar tastes good
Cinnamon to taste
Raspberry to taste

COOKING INSTRUCTION:
- Mix the tofu with a fork into a small crumb.
- Rub the banana on a small grater to make mashed potatoes or use a fork and mix with tofu.

- Add flour, a pinch of salt and sugar or sugar substitute, cinnamon to the mixture and mix thoroughly. Flours may need more or less depending on the humidity of the tofu and the size of the banana. Make sure that the mixture is thick enough to form cheesecakes.
- Form 6 cheesecakes, place on a heated frying pan with a small amount of oil, cover with the lid, hold for a few minutes, then turn the cheesecakes over and, without the top, for a few more minutes.
- Cooling down a little, the cheesecakes will become denser, orientate yourself to your taste.
- Serve with raspberries or other berries.

8. Vegan pancakes with apple sauce

Cook time: 1 Hour
Servings: 6

ENERGY VALUE PER SERVING:
Calories: 324kcal
Protein: 6.3 grams
Total Fat: 5.3 grams
Carbohydrates: 62.5 grams

INGREDIENTS:
4 Apple
2 cups Apple juice
1 cup Almond milk
200 g Wheat flour
3 tablespoons Sugar
2 tablespoons Flax flour
2 teaspoons Apple vinegar
2 teaspoons Baking powder
½ teaspoon Salt
1 teaspoon Vanilla extract
1 tablespoon Corn starch
Tasteful spices
2 tablespoons Maple syrup

COOKING INSTRUCTION:

- For making apple sauce. Peel apples, slice them into medium-sized dice and place them in a pot. Add a cup of apple juice, a tablespoon of starch, cinnamon teaspoon floor, maple syrup (can be replaced with sugar). Stir, put on heat, bring to a boil. When the sauce boils, reduce the heat and stew for 20 minutes, stirring periodically. Remove from the fire. When the apples become soft, part of the apples will stretch slightly to make the sauce thicker (the amount of starch and honey can also vary the density).

- For making pancakes: Mix a cup of almond milk with two teaspoons of vinegar and two tablespoons of flax flour. Leave the mixture for a while to thicken slightly.

- Sift 200 grams of wheat flour into a bowl, add two teaspoons of baking powder, the floor of a teaspoon of salt, a teaspoon of cinnamon, 3/4 teaspoon of ground ginger, 1/4 teaspoon of nutmeg, a pinch of ground cloves (add the spices to taste, but do not spare: fresh pancakes by themselves).

- In the flour, make a hole; pour into it a milk mixture, two tablespoons of apple sauce, 2/3 cups of apple juice, sugar, and vanilla extract. Mix everything slightly with a fork and leave the dough to rest.
- Fry on a hot pan in the usual way for you.
- Serve with apple sauce and any sour berries.

9. Coconut oatmeal with apple and maple syrup

Cook time: 15 Minutes
Servings: 1

ENERGY VALUE PER SERVING:
Calories: 227 kcal
Protein: 5.2 grams
Total Fat: 3.3 grams
Carbohydrates: 42.6 grams

INGREDIENTS:
3 tablespoons Oatmeal flakes
100 ml Coconut milk
1 tablespoon Coconut shavings
The flax seeds are a pinch
Purified pumpkin seeds are a pinch
½ Apple
Maple syrup to taste

COOKING INSTRUCTION:
- Mix oat flakes with seeds, pour water in a pot: 1/2 and bring to boil
- Add coconut milk and cook on low heat for 5 minutes stirring periodically
- Cut half of the apple finely and add it to the porridge together with the coconut chips. Cook for another 5 minutes.
- Put oatmeal in a plate, pour maple syrup.

10. Green energy cocktail

Cook time: 10 Minutes
Servings: 3

ENERGY VALUE PER SERVING:
Calories: 959kcal
Protein: 33 grams
Total Fat: 80.1 grams
Carbohydrates: 26.3 grams

INGREDIENTS:
480 g Almonds
3 cups Water
1 Bananas
1 teaspoon Vanilla extract
1 tablespoon Blue-green algae
Nutmeg pinch

COOKING INSTRUCTION:
- Soak the almonds for 8 hours in water.
- Please, mix almonds and one glass of water. Mix it in a blender.
- Mix 3 cups of almond milk, banana, and vanilla in the blender until homogeneous.
- Add the algae and stir again quickly.
- Pour the cocktail into glasses and sprinkle with nutmeg.

11. Greek manna pudding

Cook time: 30 Minutes
Servings: 3

ENERGY VALUE PER SERVING:
Calories: 368kcal
Protein: 3.5 grams
Total Fat: 16.1 grams
Carbohydrates: 53.4 grams

INGREDIENTS:
⅓-cup Manna grits
1 tablespoon Olive oil
1 tablespoon Flakes of almonds
1 tablespoon Sunflower unrefined oil
2 Dried dates
1 teaspoon sesame seeds
1 ½-cup Water
½ cup Brown sugar
1 tablespoon Orange juice
1 teaspoon Orange cedar
1 Cinnamon sticks
1 Cardamom pod
1-piece Clove
1 teaspoon Shredded ginger
Ground cinnamon to taste

COOKING INSTRUCTION:

- Combine water, sugar, orange juice and zest, clove, one crushed cardamom pod, grated ginger, and cinnamon stick in a saucepan. Place on medium heat, bring to the boil. Turn the heat down to low heat, stir and cook on low heat for about 9-10 minutes. Remove the syrup from the fire, carefully remove the cinnamon stick, and a box of cardamom — cool down at room temperature.

- Please, heat a pan with a thick bottom, add olive and sunflower oil without refining. Heat the oil and gently spray the semolina with a trickle. Intervene with almond flakes, sesame, and dates that have been soaked and cut into small pieces. Fry the grits with constant stirring for approx. 10 minutes until golden. Do not overcook the cereal; otherwise, it will be bitter.

- When the semolina becomes golden, gently and gradually intervene in the syrup, mixing it quickly and continuously. Beat the mixture until it thickens. When the mixture becomes very viscous, please remove it from the fire and cover it with a clean towel. Leave for 10 minutes. After that, spread out the crepes and send them to the fridge overnight. Serve with ground cinnamon or add a spoonful of honey.

12. Flax porridge with blueberry and chocolate chip

Cook time: 10 Minutes
Servings: 2

ENERGY VALUE PER SERVING:
Calories: 230kcal
Protein: 12.2 grams
Total Fat: 5.1 grams
Carbohydrates: 38.1 grams

INGREDIENTS:
4 tablespoons Flax porridge
1 Bananas
1 Peaches
1 teaspoon Maple syrup
1 teaspoon Sugar powder with vanilla
300ml Water
Blueberries to taste
1 teaspoon Chocolate chips

COOKING INSTRUCTION:

- Pour linen porridge into a deep bowl, pour hot water, and whip in a blender for 30 seconds.
- Add a banana to the bowl. Beat up for another 5-10 seconds. Then stir the maple syrup.
- Cut the peach into cubes. Rub the chocolate on the grater into the chips.
- Place the porridge on a plate, peach, and blueberry (preferably chilled). Sprinkle sugar powder and chocolate chips.

13. Beans and nuts

Cook time: 30 Minutes
Servings: 4

ENERGY VALUE PER SERVING:
Calories: 102kcal
Protein: 3.1 grams
Total Fat: 8.2 grams
Carbohydrates: 5.6 grams

INGREDIENTS:
1 cup Beans
50g Walnuts
1 Onion
50g Green onions

COOKING INSTRUCTION:
- Try the beans, rinse them, soak them in cold water, then drain the water, pour the beans again with cold water and boil them. Then add the finely chopped onions to the beans and let them boil.
- Shred the walnut kernel, add it to the beans, sprinkle with salt, pepper, and stir with a wooden spoon.
- Put the prepared beans in a salad bowl or deep porcelain dish and sprinkle with chopped herbs before serving.

TIP TO THE RECIPE:
Beans and nuts can be served hot and cold.

14. Tropical oatmeal in a jar

Cook time: 40 Minutes
Servings: 2

ENERGY VALUE PER SERVING:
Calories: 462kcal
Protein: 12.1 grams
Total Fat: 12.2 grams
Carbohydrates: 78.9 grams

INGREDIENTS:
100 ml Milk
150g Oatmeal flakes
200ml Canned mango
100g Canned pineapple
1 tablespoon Coconut shavings
1 tablespoon Buckwheat honey
Cinnamon on the tip of the knife
100ml Water
Vanillin on the tip of the knife

COOKING INSTRUCTION:

- Add oatmeal, milk, and water to the pot (you can add mango and pineapple juice instead of water), bring it to the boil, cook for 5 minutes, add cinnamon, and vanilla. Stir, remove from the fire.
- Cut the mango into cubes, add some to the oatmeal. Cut the pineapples into cubes and add everything to the oatmeal and cover with coconut chips. Stir, place in a jar, close the lid tightly. Allow infusing for 10 minutes.
- Honey and mango slices served separately.

Chapter 5 Vegan recipes for drinks

1. Strawberry and almond smoothies

Cook time: 30 Minutes
Servings: 4

ENERGY VALUE PER SERVING:
Calories: 132kcal
Protein: 4.2 grams
Total Fat: 7 grams
Carbohydrates: 13.8 grams

INGREDIENTS:
10 Strawberries
1 cup Almond milk
120 g Soft tofu
2 tablespoons Sugar

COOKING INSTRUCTION:
- Mix: strawberries, almond milk, tofu and sugar in a blender.
- Whisk to a homogeneous mixture.
- Pour in glasses and serve.

2. Berry and banana smoothies

Cook time: 30 Minutes
Servings: 4

ENERGY VALUE PER SERVING:
Calories: 115kcal
Protein: 2.5 grams
Total Fat: 1 grams
Carbohydrates: 25.2 grams

INGREDIENTS:
1.25 cups Orange juice
1 Bananas
1 cup Frozen berries
2 Ice pieces
50g soft tofu
1 tablespoon Sugar

COOKING INSTRUCTION:
- Mix: orange juice, peeled and sliced banana, berries, tofu, ice, and sugar in a blender (optional).
- Whisk the homogeneous mixture and serve immediately.

3.Cranberry Morse

Cook time: 40 Minutes
Servings: 12

ENERGY VALUE PER SERVING:
Calories: 142kcal
Protein: 0.2 grams
Total Fat: 0 grams
Carbohydrates: 36.1 grams

INGREDIENTS:
½ kg Cranberries
400 g Sugar
3 l. Water

COOKING INSTRUCTION:
- The cranberry is mine, and we try it out if it's fresh, or we defrost it if it's frozen.
- Put the cranberry in sieve/dishrag/multiple layers of gauze and stretch it well with a jerk or hands.
- The resulting juice is put aside, what is left of the berries - in a pot, pour cold water and sugar.
- We bring to a boil; boil for 10-15 minutes.
- Remove from the fire; pour into the pot the juice received earlier, stirred.

- We strain through a small sieve or through gauze.
- It turns out to be an excellent, saturated, to the extent of sweet morsel. For those who like to drink hot a morsel - I recommend to put a spoon of honey in a mug with morsel, so the drink will be even more useful and aromatic.

4. Banana-pear smoothies

Cook time: 10 Minutes
Servings: 2

ENERGY VALUE PER SERVING:
Calories: 353kcal
Protein: 6.2 grams
Total Fat: 1 grams
Carbohydrates: 89.3 grams

INGREDIENTS:
2 Pears
3 Bananas
2 Celery stem

COOKING INSTRUCTION:
- Mix: bananas, pears, and celery with 1 cup of water in the blender.
- Beat up to a homogeneous state.

5. Basilica drink

Cook time: 15 Minutes
Servings: 6

ENERGY VALUE PER SERVING:
Calories:102kcal
Protein: 0.3 grams
Total Fat: 0.1 grams
Carbohydrates: 25.7 grams

INGREDIENTS:
1 Red basil bundle
1 Lemon
2.5 L Water
150g Sugar

COOKING INSTRUCTION:
- Boil water in a pot. Separate the leaves from the stems of the basil and cut the lemon into rings.
- After the water has boiled, add basil, lemon, and sugar to the pot. When the water boils a second time, cover the drink with a lid and let it stand for 15 minutes.
- Please, take out the lemon so that it does not give bitterness and let it infuse for another 30 minutes.
- Sift the drink through the sieve. Drink chilled (ice-covered) or warm.

6. Drink from persimmon

Cook time: 15 Minutes
Servings: 6

ENERGY VALUE PER SERVING:
Calories: 367kcal
Protein: 11.4 grams
Total Fat: 27 grams
Carbohydrates: 23.8 grams
INGREDIENTS:
320g Almonds
6 Dates
3 cups Mineral water
3 Persimmon
½teaspoon Nutmeg
½ teaspoon Ground cinnamon
¼ teaspoon Cardamom
¼ teaspoon Ginger

COOKING INSTRUCTION:
- Soak the nuts for 8-12 hours in water.
- Mix: nuts, dates, and water in a blender until creamy.
- Put the mixture in gauze and let it flow into a bowl.
- Return the almond milk to the blender and add the remaining ingredients.
- Mix well for about 30 seconds and serve.

7. Berry drink

Cook time: 15 Minutes
Servings: 2

ENERGY VALUE PER SERVING:
Calories: 332kcal
Protein: 5.2 grams
Total Fat: 1.1 grams
Carbohydrates: 78.4 grams

INGREDIENTS:
5 Date fruit
2 Bananas
150g Strawberries
90g Raspberry
1 cup Orange juice

COOKING INSTRUCTION:
- Soak the dates for 20 minutes in water.
- In a blender, mix 1 banana, dates, and the water in which they were soaked, berries, and orange juice.

TIP TO THE RECIPE:
If the mixture is very thick, add some water and, if very liquid, some banana.

8. Layered Vegetable Fresh

Cook time: 15 Minutes
Servings: 4

ENERGY VALUE PER SERVING:
Calories: 251kcal
Protein: 5.2 grams
Total Fat: 1.5 grams
Carbohydrates: 53.8 grams

INGREDIENTS:
4 Beets
6 Apple
4 Carrots

COOKING INSTRUCTION:
- Vegetables to wash and brush thoroughly. Cut into pieces of sufficient size.
- Place a glass under the spout of the juicer, squeeze the juice out of the carrot part, then the beets over the carrot layer, then out of the apple part
- Repeat the sequence with three more Servings
- Decorate with fresh greenery

TIP TO THE RECIPE:

It is better to follow this sequence - the apples will clean the juicer from bright beetroot. You can squeeze three types of juice separately, but the effect of the layers will be different - the foam from the small cake, obtained by squeezing the juice directly into the glass, will not mix the layers.

9. Almond milk

Cook time: 30 Minutes
Servings: 8

ENERGY VALUE PER SERVING:
Calories: 537kcal
Protein: 12.2 grams
Total Fat: 31.3 grams
Carbohydrates: 54.2 grams

INGREDIENTS:
500g Almonds
400g Sugar
1 L Still mineral water

COOKING INSTRUCTION:
- Grind almonds into powder in a blender. Then mix it with the sugar and pour in water. Leave the drink in the fridge for two days.
- Run the cooled liquid through the sieve after two days.
- It is recommended to add ice to the drink before serving.

TIP TO THE RECIPE:
In the Middle Ages, almond milk was often used in cooking as a substitute for cow's milk, as its shelf life without a refrigerator is longer than that of animal milk. It could also be used during checkpoints.

10. Berry smoothies with apple juice

Cook time: 30 Minutes
Servings: 4

ENERGY VALUE PER SERVING:
Calories: 65kcal
Protein: 1.9 grams
Total Fat: 1 grams
Carbohydrates: 13,1 grams

INGREDIENTS:
½ Bananas
½cup Apple juice
1 cup Frozen berries
50g soft tofu

COOKING INSTRUCTION:
- Mix: berries, peeled and sliced bananas, apple juice, and tofu in a blender.
- Whisk to the homogeneous mixture and serve immediately.

11. Kiwi smoothies

Cook time: 5 Minutes
Servings: 4

ENERGY VALUE PER SERVING:
Calories: 75kcal
Protein: 0.9 grams
Total Fat: 0.3 grams
Carbohydrates: 17.3 grams

INGREDIENTS:
2 Kiwi
⅓ Pineapple
1 Lemon
One tablespoon Fructose

COOKING INSTRUCTION:
- Clean the lemon from the peels and films; remove the pips.
- Cut kiwi and pineapple into slices.
- Fold the fruit and ice into a blender, add fructose and whisk at high speed.
- Pour over high glasses.

TIP TO THE RECIPE:
Kiwi's better off getting fresh ones. If they are hard, it is better not to use lemon, but to make a drink of three kiwis and a specified amount of pineapple.

12. Watermelon juice with mint

Cook time: 30 Minutes
Servings: 4

ENERGY VALUE PER SERVING:
Calories: 62kcal
Protein: 1.6 grams
Total Fat: 0.3 grams
Carbohydrates: 14.6 grams

INGREDIENTS:
1 kg Watermelon
2 Fresh mint stem

COOKING INSTRUCTION:
- Clean the watermelon flesh from bones and peels.
- In the juicer, squeeze the juice out of watermelon pulp and mint. Mix and serve with ice.

13. Mint and pineapple frappe

Cook time: 15 minutes
Servings: 4

ENERGY VALUE PER SERVING:
Calories: 251kcal
Protein: 2.2 grams
Total Fat: 1.1 grams
Carbohydrates: 54 grams

INGREDIENTS:
2 kg Pineapple
1 Fresh mint bundle
40g Ice

COOKING INSTRUCTION:
- Clean the pineapple and cut it with large slices.
- Grind the ice.
- Beat ice, pineapple, and peppermint in a blender into a homogenous mass (leave some peppermint).
- Pour into glasses, decorate with mint and serve.

14. Hot milk chocolate with peppermint

Cook time: 15 minutes
Servings: 1

ENERGY VALUE PER SERVING:
Calories: 451kcal
Protein: 12.5 grams
Total Fat: 27 grams
Carbohydrates: 41.4 grams

INGREDIENTS:
250 ml Milk
50g Milk chocolate
1 Peppermint bundle

COOKING INSTRUCTION:
- Heat the milk over medium heat.
- Add the chocolate chopped into small pieces and bring it to a homogeneous state.
- Add the peppermint and mix.
- Pour the finished drink into cups.

15. Soybean milk on mineral water

Cook time: 40 minutes
Servings: 5

ENERGY VALUE PER SERVING:
Calories: 151kcal
Protein: 13 grams
Total Fat: 6.9 grams
Carbohydrates: 6.9g grams

INGREDIENTS:
1 cup Soybeans
   8   cups Mineral water

COOKING INSTRUCTION:
- Soak soybeans in three glasses of mineral water overnight.
- In the morning, move the beans into a deep bowl with the water in which they were soaked and shred with a blender. Add another three glasses of water and mix to obtain a homogeneous bean paste.

- Put the legume into the gauze and squeeze out as much liquid as possible. Put the remaining beans (pomace) of gauze back in the blender, add two more glasses of mineral water, and mix to get a homogeneous mixture. Squeeze through the gauze again and mix all the milk. Boil the raw soya milk. On high heat, bring to the boil first, stirring constantly, and then turn down the heat and cook for 5-8 minutes.
- To reduce the amount of foam, add a few drops of cold water.
- The finished milk should be filtered through the gauze and boiled again. You can add sugar, honey, chocolate, fruit, or something else.
- Chill the milk and enjoy it.

16. Grapefruit and carrot juice

Cook time: 6 minutes
Servings: 2

ENERGY VALUE PER SERVING:
Calories: 301kcal
Protein: 7.7 grams
Total Fat: 2 grams
Carbohydrates: 63.6 grams

INGREDIENTS:
2 Grapefruit
1-piece Lemon
2 Apple
7 Young carrots s
½ teaspoon Ground cinnamon
1 Ginger root

COOKING INSTRUCTION:
- Cut all the ingredients and squeeze the juice.
- Pour in glasses and sprinkle a little cinnamon.

Chapter 6 Salads

1. Salad with quinoa and yams

Cook time: 25 Minutes
Servings: 4

ENERGY VALUE PER SERVING:
Calories: 755kcal
Protein: 15.3 grams
Total Fat: 52.3 grams
Carbohydrates: 55 grams

INGREDIENTS:
240g Quinoa
200g mixture of salad leaves
200g Sweet potatoes
240g Cherry tomatoes
2 Avocado
4 Lemon slice
100g Sunflower seedlings
50ml Olive oil extra virgin
1 tablespoon Olive oil
50g Tamari sauce

COOKING INSTRUCTION:

- Boil the movie until ready (this will take about 15 minutes).
- Cut the sweet potatoes into slices of centimeter-thick slices. Grill the frying pan with a spoonful of olive oil.
- Place the lettuce leaves (Rossa, lettuce, corn, arugula, chard) on the plates. Warm quinoa on top (cold in hot weather). Then tomatoes (cut in half) and sunflower seedlings.
- Mix the salad olive oil and tamari and season the salad with sauce.
- Add lemon slices, yams, avocado slices.

2. Salad with fried tofu and sesame

Cook time: 30 Minutes
Servings: 3

ENERGY VALUE PER SERVING:
Calories: 585kcal
Protein: 35.3 grams
Total Fat: 27.4 grams
Carbohydrates: 45.4 grams

INGREDIENTS:
130g Mixed salad
200g Tofu
150g Flour for tempura
2 Cucumbers
2 Red peppers
1 Red onions
60g Basilica
1 Lemon
20ml Soy sauce
1 tablespoon Brown sugar
50ml Sesame oil
1 tablespoon Sesame
A mix of "Five peppers" to taste
Chili peppers taste good.
1 Oranges

COOKING INSTRUCTION:

- Sweet pepper to send to the oven heated up to 180 degrees, with grill function, for 20 minutes.
- Cut onions into straws, clean cucumbers and cut into half rings. Cut the basilica into large pieces. Take the pepper out of the oven, remove it from the skin and cut it into straws.
- For the dressing, mix soy sauce, lemon and orange juices, sesame oil, chili flakes, and a mixture of peppers.
- Fry the sesame a little in the pan. Mix the prepared vegetables with the dressing.
- Mix tempura with water in 1/1 ratio, add turmeric. The consistency should be similar to pancake dough.
- Cut tofu into large bars, collapse in starch, then immerse it in tempura and fry it in boiling oil until brown.
- Put the roasted tofu on a salad cushion, sprinkle with sesame, and serve immediately.

3. Spinach salad

Cook time: 10 Minutes
Servings: 2

ENERGY VALUE PER SERVING:
Calories: 191kcal
Protein: 6.5 grams
Total Fat: 16.6 grams
Carbohydrates: 5.5 grams

INGREDIENTS:
1 Spinach bundle
two tablespoons Lemon juice
two tablespoons Sharpened walnuts
1 Garlic tooth
one teaspoon Soy sauce

COOKING INSTRUCTION:
- Rinse the spinach and scald with boiling water - it should not be too small. Then rinse under cold water and place it on a plate.
- Mix lemon juice and soy sauce, add walnuts and squeeze out the garlic slice. Mix everything thoroughly, season with spinach leaves.

4. Salad with beets, baked pumpkin, and avocado

Cook time: 1 Hour
Servings: 3

ENERGY VALUE PER SERVING:
Calories: 193kcal
Protein: 5.5 grams
Total Fat: 17.6 grams
Carbohydrates: 4.5 grams

INGREDIENTS:
500g Sweet beetroot (boiled, sliced)
75g Young spinach
2 Avocado
300g Pumpkin
30g Pine nuts
30ml Olive oil
20ml Balsamic vinegar
½ Lemon
Balsamic cream to taste
Black pepper ground to taste
Salt to taste

COOKING INSTRUCTION:

- Slice the pumpkin, splash it with olive oil and send it to the oven, heated up to 180 degrees, for forty to fifty minutes.
- In a dry pan, fry pine nuts.
- Mix the boiled beetroot sliced into a drop of olive oil and balsamic vinegar.
- Rub the baked pumpkin on a large grater, add olive oil, salt, pepper, and half of the nuts.
- Save the avocado from the bone and skin and rub it on a coarse grater. Then mix half a lemon, a drop of olive oil, salt, and pepper with the juice.
- Put spinach leaves on a plate and lay prepared vegetables on them through a cooking ring: the first beetroot, then pumpkin, again beetroot, and a layer of avocado on top. Sprinkle the salad with pine nuts and decorate with balsamic cream.

5. Warm potato salad with olives and pepper

Cook time: 40 Minutes
Servings: 6

ENERGY VALUE PER SERVING:
Calories: 332kcal
Protein: 6.5 grams
Total Fat: 18.8 grams
Carbohydrates: 33.9 grams

INGREDIENTS:
3 Garlic tooth
3 tablespoons Scalloped vinegar
1 teaspoon salt
1/4 teaspoon Chili peppers
5 tablespoons Olive oil
1.4kg Young potatoes
110g Canned pepper
0.6 cup Chopped parsley
0.3 cup Olives without pips

COOKING INSTRUCTION:

- Rinse the potatoes thoroughly and boil them in boiling salt water for about 10-15 minutes. Drain and cut in half.
- Rub garlic and a pinch of salt in the mortar to a paste. Put in a large bowl and mix with vinegar, salt, and chili flakes. Beating up, enter
- Olive oil.
- Add the hot potatoes and mix well. Leave for about 30 minutes until the potatoes are warm. Then add finely sliced peppers, parsley, and sliced olives. Serve warm.

6. Salad with chickpeas and fresh vegetables

Cook time: 10 Minutes
Servings: 2

ENERGY VALUE PER SERVING:
Calories: 86kcal
Protein: 4.1 grams
Total Fat: 1.7 grams
Carbohydrates: 13.8 grams

INGREDIENTS:
1 Romance salad
1 Canned chickpea
1 Green onion bundle
1 Tomatoes
1 Sweet pepper
10g Garlic
Olive oil to taste
Salt to taste
Black pepper ground to taste
2 tablespoons Apple vinegar

COOKING INSTRUCTION:

- Wash and slice salad leaves, green onions, peppers, and tomatoes. Add garlic and chickpea and mix.
- Pour olive oil, vinegar, and brown sugar into a small jar with a lid. Add salt and pepper to taste. Shake well.
- Pour the salad dressing and stir slightly.

7. Salad with green beans and hazelnuts

Cook time: 30 Minutes
Servings: 4

ENERGY VALUE PER SERVING:
Calories: 231 kcal
Protein: 3.6 grams
Total Fat: 22.6 grams
Carbohydrates: 6.1 grams

INGREDIENTS:
30g Hazelnut
2.25 teaspoons Grainy mustard
340g Green beans
Sea salt pinch
4 teaspoons Olive oil
1.5 teaspoons Balsamic vinegar
1 tablespoon Cold-pressed linseed oil
1 teaspoon Hazelnut butter
60g Red onions

COOKING INSTRUCTION:

- Heat the oven to 160 degrees.
- Place the nuts on a baking tray and fry to the golden middle for about 15-20 minutes. Check by breaking the nut. Cooldown a little and chop the knife into small pieces.
- Bring the salt water to the boil in a large pan. Place the beans cut into small pieces diagonally and boil for about 4-6 minutes until soft. Drain and quickly transfer to ice or rinse under cold water.
- Mix: mustard, vinegar, and salt in a bowl. Then add the olive, linen, and hazelnut oil. Lightly whisk and add beans, nuts, and finely sliced onions.
- Mix well, salt and pepper.

8. Cauliflower salad with pepper and olives

Cook time: 30 Minutes
Servings: 4

ENERGY VALUE PER SERVING:
Calories: 165kcal
Protein: 3 grams
Total Fat: 13 grams
Carbohydrates: 8.1 grams

INGREDIENTS:
2 tablespoons Wine vinegar
300g Cauliflower cabbage
1 Sweet pepper
5 Olives
3 tablespoons Vegetable oil
1 Parsley bundle
Mixed peppers to taste
Salt to taste

COOKING INSTRUCTION:

- Disassemble the cauliflower into inflorescences, boil it in saltwater and spray it with wine vinegar.
- Slice the peppers into straws.
- Whisk the vegetable oil and wine vinegar and add the chopped olives and herbs for the filling.
- Combine cauliflower, pepper, and season with salad. Pour salt, pepper.

9. Orange and avocado salad

Cook time: 15 Minutes
Servings: 2

ENERGY VALUE PER SERVING:
Calories: 431kcal
Protein: 6.4 grams
Total Fat: 36.4 grams
Carbohydrates: 23.1 grams

INGREDIENTS:
1 Orange
1 Avocado
½ Fennel
Green salad to taste
Lemon juice to taste
Sea salt pinch
Freshly ground black pepper to taste
40g Pine nuts

COOKING INSTRUCTION:
- Cut the fennel into thin strips and, after placing it on a plate, pour lemon juice and salt a little. Cut the avocado in half, cut the skin and slice it into half a centimeter-thick slices. Also, pour it with lemon juice and add some salt. Cut the orange peeled in half and slice it into slices.
- Place the salad leaves (iceberg, Rosso logo, or oak salad) on the bottom of the plate, with fennel, avocado, and orange on them. Mix gently, sprinkle black pepper and pine nuts. For brightness, decorate with strips of fresh carrot or red pepper.

10. Wild rice salad

Cook time: 1 Hour 10 Minutes
Servings: 4

ENERGY VALUE PER SERVING:
Calories: 181kcal
Protein: 4.7 grams
Total Fat: 10.7 grams
Carbohydrates: 17.5 grams

INGREDIENTS:
1.5 cups Wild rice
2 tablespoons Sesame oil
200 g Green beans
200 g Butter beans
1 Lemon
2 Garlic cloves

COOKING INSTRUCTION:

- Pour 1 1/2 cups of wild rice into 4 cups of slightly salted water, bring to the boil, after turning off the heat and keeping for about 40-50 minutes. It should become soft, and most of the drawings "open."
- Ideally, the rice should be soaked for an hour or two in hot water and boiled with 3 glasses of water for the same 40-50 minutes.
- Boil the beans (green and yellow) in water for no more than 5 minutes or cook in a steamer.
- Cut the garlic as finely as possible or squeeze it out with a presser. Cut onions into thin half-rings.
- Remove the zest from the lemon and squeeze out the juice. Mix garlic, zest, 1/2 lemon juice with sesame oil.
- I am dressing the resulting sauce with rice and beans.
- Serve hot with soy sauce!
- You can add pieces of goat cheese or mozzarella.
- Consume with pleasure and, if possible, with sticks.

11. Asian salad with orange, spinach, and avocado

Cook time: 15 Minutes
Servings: 4

ENERGY VALUE PER SERVING:
Calories: 215kcal
Protein: 3.3 grams
Total Fat: 17.9 grams
Carbohydrates: 12.4 grams

INGREDIENTS:
180g Young spinach
1 Oranges
1 Avocado
30 g Shallot
10g Ginger root
2 tablespoons Rice vinegar
1 tablespoon Vegetable oil
¼ teaspoon Sesame oil
Salt to taste
Black pepper ground to taste

COOKING INSTRUCTION:

- It is enough to finely cut the shawl, crush ginger, mix, add vinegar and oil - sesame and tablespoon of the plant - Whip, salt, and pepper the filling.
- Clean the orange from the peel and white layer under it, cut in circles about 1 cm thick, and divide each circle in two. Cut avocado into thin slices.
- Mix the spinach with the dressing and then with the avocado and orange, gently overturn the salad and serve.

12. Avocado, tomato and basil salad

Cook time: 30 Minutes
Servings: 4

ENERGY VALUE PER SERVING:
Calories: 314kcal
Protein: 5.4 grams
Total Fat: 28.5 grams
Carbohydrates: 12.9 grams

INGREDIENTS:
4 cups Romano salad
4 Tomatoes
1 Avocado
¼ Red onions
12 Olives without pips
8 Basil leaves
Six tablespoons Italian salad dressing

COOKING INSTRUCTION:
- In a large bowl, place the salad leaves torn into small pieces.
- Slice small pieces of tomatoes, also thin, slice onions in half rings.
- Slice avocado in cubes.
- Cut olives and basil leave into circles.
- Spray the salad with dressing and stir.

TIP TO THE RECIPE:
This salad is great for pasta, pizza, and risotto.

Chapter 7 Vegan soup recipes

1. Tomato cream soup with dried tomatoes

Cook time: 40 Minutes
Servings: 5

ENERGY VALUE PER SERVING:
Calories: 236kcal
Protein: 4.7 grams
Total Fat: 14.4 grams
Carbohydrates: 23.6 grams

INGREDIENTS:
185g potatoes
50g Celery
110g Carrots
130g Onion
450g Tomatoes
85g Dried tomatoes in olive oil
650ml Water
15g Garlic
65ml Olive oil
Black pepper ground to taste
Salt to taste

COOKING INSTRUCTION:

- In a large pot, heat the olive oil, fry the garlic and basil so that they give the juice back. Cut potatoes, celery, carrots and onions into large cubes, put the vegetables into a pot and stew for 10 minutes over medium heat.
- Cut tomatoes into four parts and add to the vegetables, stew until the tomatoes give away almost all the juice. Then add the dried tomatoes, Napoli sauce, salt, and pepper, and pour water. Stew until the vegetables are fully cooked, then punch everything in the blender.
- Serve ready, warm soup with olive oil and basil leaves.

2. Eggplant puree soup

Cook time: 30 Minutes
Servings: 4

ENERGY VALUE PER SERVING:
Calories: 56kcal
Protein: 2.4 grams
Total Fat: 0.2 grams
Carbohydrates: 11.9 grams

INGREDIENTS:
600g Eggplants
2 Finely chopped garlic cloves
Crushed fresh thyme to taste
Olive oil to taste
1 tablespoon Balsamic vinegar
1 Onion
500ml Water
Salt to taste

COOKING INSTRUCTION:

- Clean the aubergines from their skin and cut them into semicircular slices approximately 1 cm thick. Purify and shred the garlic clove, peel the onion and cut it into thin curved rings. Trim the leaves from the thyme branches.
- Heat the olive oil in a small pan over medium heat. Throw slices of eggplant, thyme, and pour in balsamic vinegar. Mix and add more olive oil - fry slices of eggplant on all sides.
- In a small pot, heat up some olive oil and fry chopped onions and garlic over low heat until soft (seven to ten minutes). Add the fried eggplants, add water, and bring to the boil - cook for twenty minutes with the lid on.
- Remove the pot from the fire and use a submersible blender to turn its contents into a puree. And then, if desired, wipe additionally through a sieve - for an airier consistency. Add more water or broth, if necessary, salt and pepper to taste.
- The ready-made soup can be slightly warmed up again on the fire, or it can be immediately poured on plates - it is good both in hot and warm conditions. Decorate each serving with thyme leaves and serve.

3. Gentle pumpkin puree soup

Cook time: 45 Minutes
Servings: 2

ENERGY VALUE PER SERVING:
Calories: 129kcal
Protein: 5.4 grams
Total Fat: 0.8 grams
Carbohydrates: 31.6 grams

INGREDIENTS:
300g Pumpkin
150g Celery root
150g Carrots
1 teaspoon Ginger root
1 Onion
1 Garlic tooth
Olive oil to taste
1 pcs Green pepper

COOKING INSTRUCTION:

- Cut pumpkin and carrots in large cubes, pour water on them so that the vegetables covered with water, but no more.
- Salt to taste and cook to softness.
- Onions, celery and garlic, are and fried in olive oil until golden.
- In addition to the pumpkin and carrot, we add the fried vegetables and rubbed ginger root and shred with a blender.
- Serve with cubes or strips of sweet paprika (better green), favorite herbs, as well as granulated bran or dried bread.

4. Green soup with ginger

Cook time: 35 Minutes
Servings: 4

ENERGY VALUE PER SERVING:
Calories: 251kcal
Protein: 5.2 grams
Total Fat: 15.7 grams
Carbohydrates: 25.1 grams

INGREDIENTS:
2 Onion
300g Young potatoes
150g Leek
2 Fresh spinach leaves
30g Ginger root
three tablespoons Olive oil
Sea salt to taste
150g Carrots
Black pepper ground to taste
1 l Vegetable broth

COOKING INSTRUCTION:

- Finely cut and stew the onion slowly in olive oil, stirring from time to time, over low heat until the onion becomes soft and golden. About 20-25 minutes.
- Meanwhile, peel potatoes and carrots cut them into small cubes, and immerse them in vegetable broth (or water). Please, bring it to the boil.
- Wash leek and spinach thoroughly, cut roughly.
- Cut ginger finely.
- Add onions, spinach, and ginger to boiling water with semi-finished potatoes and carrots, reduce the heat, and then keep for 5 minutes.
- Add salt and pepper to taste.
- Pour over the plates. Serve with a spoonful of golden onions on top.

5. Tomato cream soup

Cook time: 15 Minutes
Servings: 2

ENERGY VALUE PER SERVING:
Calories: 431kcal
Protein: 17.3 grams
Total Fat: 15.9 grams
Carbohydrates: 55.6 grams

INGREDIENTS:
1 cup Dried tomatoes
1 Tomatoes
2 cups Water
½ Avocado
1 Garlic tooth
Salt to taste
Lemon juice to taste

COOKING INSTRUCTION

- Soak dried tomatoes for an hour in water at room temperature.
- Purify the fresh tomatoes from the seeds, avocado from the peel, and bone.
- Shred the vegetables by adding salt and lemon juice in the blender to a homogenous state.
- Add water.
- Serve with fresh green basil leaves.
- You can make your own dried tomatoes. Use Georgian (fleshy) tomato varieties better. Cut them into circles about 1 cm thick and bake them in an oven at 100-120 C for about 3 hours.

6. Spinach and sorrel cream soup with avocado

Cook time: 10 Minutes
Servings: 2

ENERGY VALUE PER SERVING:
Calories: 412kcal
Protein: 6.5 grams
Total Fat: 35.5 grams
Carbohydrates: 21.4 grams

INGREDIENTS:
1 tablespoon Olive oil
1 Onion
1 Spinach bundle
½ Sorrel bundle
1 Avocado
2 Garlic cloves
2 cups Vegetable broth

COOKING INSTRUCTION:

- Pour the oil into the pan, stew the chopped onions until they are clear and soft.
- Wash and remove the stems from the spinach leaves. Add the finely torn leaves and broth (water) to the onions. Cook for 3-5 minutes, stirring periodically.
- Add the sorrel leaves washed and separated from the stems. Boil for another 3-5 minutes.
- Remove from the fire, add avocado and squeezed garlic, grind with a blender to a homogeneous condition.
- Serve with chopped parsley or arugula.

TIP TO THE RECIPE:

Vegetable broth can be replaced with drinking water.

7. Delphi cold fast soup

Cook time: 20 Minutes
Servings: 4

ENERGY VALUE PER SERVING:
Calories: 505kcal
Protein: 8.2 grams
Total Fat: 38.3 grams
Carbohydrates: 36.8 grams

INGREDIENTS:
5 Carrots
4 Celery stem
1/4 beetroot
3 Avocado
1 Apple
1 Fresh red pepper
2 teaspoons Curry
1 Garlic tooth
Salt to taste
2 Tomatoes
Kinza tastes good
½ Cucumbers

COOKING INSTRUCTION:
- Squeeze the juice out of carrots, beetroots, celery, and apples.
- Pour the juice into the blender and add 2 avocadoes, pepper, curry, garlic, and salt and whisk to a homogenous state.
- Cut 1 avocado, tomatoes, and cucumber into small cubes and place on plates.
- Pour in soup and sprinkle with coriander.

8. Spicy corn puree soup

Cook time: 30 Minutes
Servings: 4

ENERGY VALUE PER SERVING:
Calories: 271kcal
Protein: 7.6 grams
Total Fat: 6.8 grams
Carbohydrates: 47.3 grams

INGREDIENTS:
1 teaspoon Seeds of cumin (Zira)
1 teaspoon Coriander seeds
1 teaspoon Curcuma
1 teaspoon Chili peppers
1 teaspoon Shredded ginger
1 Garlic tooth
2 teaspoons Olive oil extra virgin
1 Onion
3 Potatoes
2 Carrots
1 L Vegetable broth
2 (two cans) Sweet Canned corn

COOKING INSTRUCTION:

- Curry pasta: Warm the seeds of cumin and coriander in a hot frying pan until aroma appears.
- Pour the grains into the mortar, rub with finely sliced garlic and ginger, turmeric, and ground chili.
- Pour the oil in small portions and stir to the pasta. A tablespoon is needed for the soup.
- Preparing the soup: slice the onions into small cubes. Fry it with curry paste in a frying pan, where the olive oil was preheated.
- Then add the carrot grated on a large grater.
- After 5 minutes, add the potatoes sliced in small cubes. Fry everything together over low heat for 10 minutes.
- Put into a pot, pour the broth, salt, and pepper.
- When the potatoes are ready, add corn puree (to do this, grind one can of corn in a blender). Also, add 100 grams of whole corn grains and bring the soup to the boil.
- Then grind the soup in the blender bowl to a homogeneous, smooth puree. Pour into a pan.
- Add the remaining whole corn grains to the mashed pot soup and warm on a stove.

9. Beet soup with coconut milk

Cook time: 40 Minutes
Servings: 4

ENERGY VALUE PER SERVING:
Calories: 195kcal
Protein: 3.4 grams
Total Fat: 12.4 grams
Carbohydrates: 19.4 grams

INGREDIENTS:
1 Beets
1 Potatoes
1 Onion
1 tablespoon Vegetable oil
½ Celery stem
½ Carrots.
2 Tomatoes
1 teaspoon Shredded ginger
2 tablespoons canned corn
2 tablespoons Chopped cilantro (coriander)
1 cup Coconut milk
Salt to taste
Black pepper ground to taste

COOKING INSTRUCTION:

- Bake the beets, cool them down and peel them off. Peel the potatoes cut them into cubes, and place them in a small pot with a little water.
- Heat the oil in the pan. Add chopped onions, carrots, celery, and grated ginger and stew on low heat for a few minutes. Add sliced tomatoes, salt and continue to stew for a few more minutes. Add potatoes to the pan (along with the water in which they were cooked), close with the lid and cook over low heat for 5 minutes.
- Place the contents of the pan in a blender, add the beetroot and purée. Return the soup to the fire and stir in the coconut milk.
- Pour the soup over the plates, add some sweet corn and chopped coriander to each one.

10. Soup with carrots, coriander, apple and cabbage

Cook time: 1 Hour
Servings: 8

ENERGY VALUE PER SERVING:
Calories: 91kcal
Protein: 3.2 grams
Total Fat: 0.5 grams
Carbohydrates: 19.9 grams

INGREDIENTS:
200g Apple
400g Carrots
100g Ginger
1 Savoy cabbage
1 Onion
1 Leek stem
2 Celery stem
1 Lemon
2 Garlic cloves
3 Lemongrass stem
30g Kinza

COOKING INSTRUCTION:

- In a three-liter pot of water to put sliced into small segments of the leek, chopped onions, chopped ginger, one hundred grams of carrots, coriander roots, and lemongrass, bring to the boil, put down and cook on low heat for forty minutes.
- Sweep the ready broth, add finely chopped carrots, coarsely chopped celery, and chopped cabbage. Cook for 15 minutes, throw in the sliced green apples, and cook five more. Fill with coriander, garlic, and lemon juice and pierce the soup in a blender. The aroma and taste of soup are so rich that you can do without salt and pepper.

TIP TO THE RECIPE:

Basically, it's a "vitamin salad," shifted to the soup tongue. Additional elements such as lemongrass, garlic, ginger, and celery are needed to create a palette of flavors.

11. Carrot, broccoli and ginger soup with legumes and green onions

Cook time: 10 Minutes
Servings: 2

ENERGY VALUE PER SERVING:
Calories: 176 kcal
Protein: 7.1 grams
Total Fat: 0.8 grams
Carbohydrates: 38.3 grams

INGREDIENTS:
2 Lemon
4 Carrots
50g Broccoli cabbage
50g Legumes
2 Garlic cloves
20g Green onions
20g Ginger
¼ Red onions
1 tablespoon Maple syrup

COOKING INSTRUCTION:

- Peel carrots, cut into small pieces, and leave the carrots in the blender. Also, send two lemons of juice, some medium-sized broccoli blossoms, garlic, red and green onions, grated ginger, and maple syrup to the blender.
- Throw in a glass of drinking water and grind the blender's contents in pulse mode to produce a pleasant orange porridge in color and consistency.
- Add liquids if the porridge seems too thick. Turn again.

TIP TO THE RECIPE:

Serve this soup by adding a handful of legumes and a few green onion feathers to each plate to cheer the eye and get a few injections of extra taste and texture sensations on the teeth.

To further enhance the taste of this soup, you can add coriander leaves to it. Carrots and cilantro are a classic combination.

12. Bean soup with chili

Cook time: 50 Minutes
Servings: 2

ENERGY VALUE PER SERVING:
Calories: 205kcal
Protein: 12.4 grams
Total Fat: 1.2 grams
Carbohydrates: 38.1 grams

INGREDIENTS:
1.25 l Water
175g Red beans
175g Carrots
1 Onion.
2 Garlic cloves
½ Red chili pepper
2 Tomatoes
1 l Vegetable broth
2 Celery stem
Salt to taste
1 tablespoon Chopped parsley
Black pepper ground to taste

COOKING INSTRUCTION:

- Soak the beans overnight in cold water, then drain and place in a pot of water. Bring to the boil and cook for 10 minutes. Reduce the heat, cover with the lid, and cook for about 2 hours until the beans are ready.
- Finely slice carrots, onions, garlic, crush, pepper, and slice. Add broth and prepared vegetables to the beans, bring to the boil, cover with the lid and cook for another 30 minutes.
- Take half the vegetables out of the pot with a small amount of broth and make them puree in a blender or kitchen combine.
- Return the bean puree to the pot, add chopped and peeled tomatoes, and finely chopped celery. Stew for 10-15 minutes until the celery becomes soft, if necessary, add some water or broth.
- Salt and pepper the soup to taste. And add chopped coriander or parsley.

TIP TO THE RECIPE:

The vegetable broth should be cooked like this:
Lay a small bulb in the husk in cold water, bay leaf, pepper, green stems (freeze if necessary, in advance), then take it all out for cooking.

Chapter 8 Vegan recipes for main courses

1. Beijing cabbage with mint and green peas

Cook time: 40 Minutes
Servings: 2

ENERGY VALUE PER SERVING:
Calories: 253kcal
Protein: 6.5 grams
Total Fat: 20.5 grams
Carbohydrates: 15.2 grams

INGREDIENTS:
1/2 Peking cabbage
1 tablespoon Rice vinegar
1 tablespoon Soy sauce
1 Fresh mint bundle
2 tablespoons Sesame oil
100g Green peas
1 Chili peppers

COOKING INSTRUCTION:

- Heat the pan; pour sesame oil into it, then soy sauce and vinegar.
- Add the sliced green peas, fry for thirty seconds, then add the noodled Beijing cabbage and fry for another minute.
- At the end of this time, add the peppermint sliced in chili peppers and stir. Switch off the heat. Cover with the lid. Allow to stand for a minute and serve at the table.

TIP TO THE RECIPE:

In combination with mint in this recipe, you can use spicy herbs with a more pronounced taste, such as coriander or parsley. Rice vinegar is best cooked with white vinegar. Black, with its powerful aroma, can clog the tweak the flavor of Beijing cabbage and green peas. It is better not to overcook the vegetables, but to bring them to an al-dente state. They should be slightly crispy.

2. Stewed cabbage

Cook time: 40 Minutes
Servings: 4

ENERGY VALUE PER SERVING:
Calories: 147kcal
Protein: 3.2 grams
Total Fat: 9.2 grams
Carbohydrates: 13,6 grams

INGREDIENTS:
1 Onion
½ kg White cabbage
½ tablespoon Vinegar
½ tablespoon Sugar
½tablespoon Wheat flour
1 tablespoon Tomato puree
½ cup Water
2 tablespoons Vegetable oil

COOKING INSTRUCTION:

- Shred the cleaned cabbage and put it into a pot, add oil and water, cover with a lid and stew for 20 minutes.
- Cut and fry the onion, add it to the cabbage, then put the tomato puree, vinegar, sugar, season to taste, and continue to stew.
- When the cabbage is ready, add the oil-fried flour, stir and boil.

3. Lentils with mushrooms

Cook time: 30 Minutes
Servings: 4

ENERGY VALUE PER SERVING:
Calories: 115kcal
Protein: 9.2 grams
Total Fat: 1.1 grams
Carbohydrates: 21 grams

INGREDIENTS:
1 cup Lentils
300g Fresh champignons
2 Onion
2 Garlic cloves
1 Carrots
Salt to taste
Parsley tastes good
Black pepper ground to taste
Dill to taste

COOKING INSTRUCTION:

- Lentils should be washed well and placed in a pot. Pour lentils 2.5-3 glasses of water, put on fire, and bring to the boil.
- After boiling, reduce the fire, salt and boil, taking off the foam for about 20 minutes, until the lentils are soft, but will retain their shape. If, after cooking, not all the liquid is absorbed into the lentils, it can be drained.
- Clean the onions and cut them finely. Clean the garlic and chop it.
- Wash the carrots, clean them, and rub them on a coarse grater. Wash the champignons and slice them.
- In a heated pan with oil, fry onions and garlic until soft for 1-2 minutes.
- Add the carrots and fry, occasionally stirring for about 3 minutes.
- Place the mushrooms and cook, stirring periodically for 8 minutes until ready.
- Add boiled lentils to the mushrooms in the pan.
- Put the chopped herbs in the pan.
- Pour salt, pepper to taste, and mix lentils with mushrooms.

TIP TO THE RECIPE:

Garlic can be added at the very end of the frying process to make the dish spicier.

4. Zucchini ratatouille

Cook time: 1 Hour
Servings 3

ENERGY VALUE PER SERVING:
Calories: 351kcal
Protein: 3.4 grams
Total Fat: 24.6 grams
Carbohydrates: 29.2 grams

INGREDIENTS:
Salt to taste
2 pieces' Green pepper
1 teaspoon Sugar
1 kg Tomatoes
250g Onion
7 tablespoons Olive oil
2 kg Courgettes

COOKING INSTRUCTION:

- Cut onion and tomatoes. Cut the peeled zucchini and peppers into cubes - don't forget to remove the seeds from the zucchini. Heat 3 tablespoons of oil in a pot, add onions, and cook over low heat, stirring for 5 minutes until the onions are transparent. Add the zucchini and cook for another five minutes, stirring until it also starts to fry.
- Heat 2 spoons of oil in a pan, add the tomatoes and cook over low heat, sometimes stirring for 10 minutes. Let them cool down, then whisk them in a blender in mashed potatoes, sprinkle salt and sugar and pour on the zucchini; mix them all. Cook over low heat for another 25 minutes, adding some water if the mixture seems too thick.
- In a tomato-free pan, heat up 2 tablespoons of butter, add peppers, cover with a lid and leave on low heat for 25 minutes, stirring sometimes. Then intervene in the zucchini and serve immediately in a heated deep dish.

TIP TO THE RECIPE:

This dish can be cooked in advance and warmed up. You can also whip up the ready-made ratatouille in a blender, and add three whipped eggs before serving and serve with triangular pieces of toasted bread.

5. Pumpkin curry with chickpea and zucchini

Cook time: 45 Minutes
Servings: 6

ENERGY VALUE PER SERVING:
Calories: 435kcal
Protein: 23.4 grams
Total Fat: 8.3 grams
Carbohydrates: 70.9 grams

INGREDIENTS:
500g Pumpkin
1 cups red lentils
400g Nut
2 pieces Zucchini
1 Onion
1 Garlic tooth
2 teaspoons Curry
1 L Vegetable broth
500g Cauliflower cabbage
Fresh coriander
1 tablespoon Vegetable oil

COOKING INSTRUCTION:

- Clean the raw pumpkin from the peel and cut it into cubes of 3x3 cm2. Throw finely sliced onions, garlic, curry, pumpkin into a large pot of heated vegetable oil, and stir for 3 minutes over high heat.
- Add pre-prepared (or canned) lentils and vegetable broth to the pot. Bring the mixture to the boil.
- Reduce the heat and continue to cook over medium heat until the pumpkin is soft (approx. 5 minutes). Fall asleep in a saucepan with pumpkin and lentils sliced in cubes of zucchini, precooked chickpea and cauliflower divided into inflorescences - cook over medium heat for 5 minutes.
- Remove from the fire and season with salt and pepper to taste. Sprinkle the dish with fresh coriander before serving.

6. Eggplants by Greek

Cook time: 30 Minutes
Servings: 2

ENERGY VALUE PER SERVING:
Calories: 382kcal
Protein: 2.6 grams
Total Fat: 36.2 grams
Carbohydrates: 12g grams

INGREDIENTS:
120g Eggplants
One teaspoon Wheat flour
Green onions to taste
20g Spinach
Four tablespoons Vegetable oil
1 Tomatoes
Green salad to taste
Salt to taste
1 Sweet pepper

COOKING INSTRUCTION:
- Clean the aubergines and cut them into 1 cm thick circles. Roll each one in flour and fry in hot vegetable oil.

- Cut green onions, spinach, bell pepper, parsley and tomatoes, salt, and pass over medium heat in vegetable oil for 5 minutes.
- Place the eggplant in the baking dish.
- Pour the roasted vegetable mix and sweat in the oven for 10-15 minutes. Decorate with chopped herbs and serve cold.

7. Garlic ratatouille

Cook time: **2 Hours**
Serving: 6

ENERGY VALUE PER SERVING:
Calories: 324kcal
Protein: 5.4 grams
Total Fat: 25.6 grams
Carbohydrates: 21.2 grams

INGREDIENTS:
Salt to taste
2 Garlic cloves
500g Tomatoes
Four pieces Zucchini
Two pieces' Green pepper
Three pieces Eggplant
300g Onion
150 ml Olive oil

COOKING INSTRUCTION:

- Finely cut the onions. Cleans zucchini and eggplant from skin and seeds - cut into cubes. Remove the seeds from the peppers and also cut them into cubes. Tomatoes should be stripped of their skins and finely chopped.
- Heat the olive oil in a large deep pan. Send onions there and cook on low heat, stirring for 10 minutes. Add the eggplant and cook for another 10 minutes.
- Pour in the pepper, stir and cook for another 10 minutes. Add zucchini and tomatoes, garlic, and salt. Cover with the lid and leave on low heat for 1 hour.
- If the vegetable juice is too much, open the lid for 10 minutes to allow the excess moisture to evaporate.
- Remove the garlic cloves before serving.

8. Vegetarian pilaf with chickpea

Cook time: 45 Minutes
Servings: 3

ENERGY VALUE PER SERVING:
Calories: 981kcal
Protein: 17.1 grams
Total Fat: 53.8 grams
Carbohydrates: 111.1 grams

INGREDIENTS:
1 cup Fig
½ Carrots
½ Onion
½ cup. Nut
1 teaspoon Cumin (Zira)
50 ml Vegetable oil
1 tablespoon Barbarians
3 Garlic tooth
Sea salt to taste
Black pepper ground to taste
2 cups Water

COOKING INSTRUCTION:

- Cut large onions.
- Grind carrots on the grater.
- Boil the chickpea beforehand until it is half ready.
- Pour oil into the wok (deep pan), generously to cover the bottom.
- Layout the onions first, then the carrots, then the chickpea.
- Pour rice on top, then add the spices.
- Do not clean garlic cloves, "hide" them in pilaf in several places, one clove at a time. This will give an exquisite taste and aroma.
- Pour two or more glasses of water into the pilaf and place it on fire. Alternatively, please put it in a bottom-heated oven.

TIP TO THE RECIPE:

You can give up garlic, but I can't say anything about onions - only it doesn't irritate the stomach in this dish at all.

9. Buckwheat noodles with tomatoes, tofu, and basil

Cook time: 26 Minutes
Servings: 4

ENERGY VALUE PER SERVING:
Calories: 461kcal
Protein: 22.1 grams
Total Fat: 17.2 grams
Carbohydrates: 55.4 grams

INGREDIENTS:
230g Buckwheat noodles
450 g Tofu
1.5 tablespoons Olive oil
680g Tomatoes
2 teaspoons dark sesame oil
Crushed basil leaves to taste
1 teaspoon Curry powder
1 tablespoon Sugar
2 pieces' Green onions
2 tablespoons Soy sauce

COOKING INSTRUCTION:

- Prepare noodles in plenty of boiling water to al dente.
- Meanwhile, cut the tofu into 1x1 cm cubes.
- Heat the oil in a full shallow pan.
- Add tofu and fry at a medium-high temperature until most sides are golden.
- Add the tomatoes and cook until they begin to soften.
- Combine the noodles and tomato mixture with tofu.
- Add the remaining ingredients, mix well, and serve.

TIP TO THE RECIPE:

For a spicier version of this dish, add dried hot red pepper flakes, or any Asian spicy sauce you like. You can also add boiled asparagus (2-3 pieces), decorate with raw, match-sized carrots and zucchini, and sesame seeds.

10. Fried vegetables with mushrooms, sesame oil, and soy sauce

Cook time: 30 Minutes
Servings: 4

ENERGY VALUE PER SERVING:
Calories: 948kcal
Protein: 37.5 grams
Total Fat: 34.5 grams
Carbohydrates: 127.6 grams

INGREDIENTS:
250g Ramen noodles
1 l. Vegetable broth
2 Garlic cloves
2 pieces Zucchini
2 tablespoons Vegetable oil
2 stem leek
15 Fresh champignons
1/4 cup Legumes
14 pods green peas
1 Tofu
1 teaspoon salt
2 teaspoons Sugar
2 tablespoons light soy sauce
2 teaspoons Sesame oil
4 Green onions

COOKING INSTRUCTION:

- Please put the noodles in the water. Please bring it to a boil for 2-3 minutes. The noodles should become soft. Drain and rinse under cold water and arrange in 2 bowls. Heat the broth and pour it into the noodles.
- In the meantime, heat the wok over medium heat for 1-2 minutes until it is smoky and add vegetable oil. Fry the chopped garlic for 5 seconds, then add the sliced vegetables, mushrooms, and tofu, but do not combine the green onions. Fry for 2-3 minutes until soft.
- Add salt, sugar, and soy sauce, then spray with sesame oil. Place on noodles and sprinkle with green onions.

11. Idaho potatoes

Cook time: 1 Hour
Servings: 3

ENERGY VALUE PER SERVING:
Calories: 974kcal
Protein: 9.5 grams
Total Fat: 84.7 grams
Carbohydrates: 46.1 grams

INGREDIENTS:
10 Young potatoes
250 ml Olive oil extra virgin
1 Dill bundle
1 Parsley bundle
3 Garlic tooth
1 teaspoon Red tabasco sauce
Salt to taste

COOKING INSTRUCTION:
- Rinse the potatoes thoroughly (do not peel), cut them into eight slices, place them in a pot with cold, salty water.
- Bring to the boil and cook for 2-3 minutes. Drain the water and cool down the potatoes.

- Mix the olive oil with finely chopped herbs, sauce, and garlic squeezed through the garlic crusher. Place the potatoes on a baking tray in one layer, dipping the slices into the resulting mixture.
- Please, Bake in the oven for 15-20 minutes at 200 degrees Celsius.

TIP TO THE RECIPE:
I recommend using a non-stick-coated tray or, if a standard tray is used, place parchment under the potatoes.

12. Vegetarian chili in Mexican

Cook time: 40 Minutes
Servings: 4

ENERGY VALUE PER SERVING:
Calories: 351kcal
Protein: 16.4 grams
Total Fat: 10.2 grams
Carbohydrates: 49.5 grams

INGREDIENTS:
- Peel and slice vegetables - onions, bell peppers, and celery. Cut the garlic finely.
- Tomatoes for this recipe can be used both fresh and sliced, which sold in shops. I used sliced Pomito tomatoes. Fresh tomatoes need to be sliced into small cubes, and the skin can't be removed.
- Heat the oil in a pan (2-3 tablespoons) - fry onions and garlic over medium heat for 3 minutes.
- Then add celery and bell pepper. Cook for another 5-7 minutes, stirring every couple of minutes.
- Add tomatoes, 1/2 cups of water, 1.5 tablespoons of tomato paste, mix well. After the liquid boils, add 1.5 tsp salt, 1-2 tsp red pepper, 1 tsp dried oregano.

- Also, add two standard cans of canned beans (white and red). Place the fire on a slow one, cover with the lid, and cook for 10 minutes.
- When serving, decorate with chopped herbs.

13. Vegan curry of chickpea and potatoes

Cook time: 25 Minutes
Servings: 4

ENERGY VALUE PER SERVING:
Calories: 335kcal
Protein: 11.4 grams
Total Fat: 11 grams
Carbohydrates: 47.8 grams

INGREDIENTS:
300g Young potatoes
2 tablespoons Curry paste
1 Onion.
3 Garlic
Cumin to taste
Curcuma to taste
The curry tastes good.
Fresh ginger to taste
Chili peppers taste good
1 tablespoon Tomato paste
2 teaspoons Sugar
½ cup Nut
2 teaspoons Starch
1 cup Coconut milk

COOKING INSTRUCTION:

- Peas chickpea soak at night. Then rinse and boil until half ready in saltwater.
- Wash the young potatoes and slice them into the rind. Fry on a heated frying pan until a golden crust is dense.
- Place potatoes, peas, curry paste (or 1 tablespoon of curry powder), crushed garlic clove, turmeric in a pot.
- Pour in coconut milk, bring to the boil, add water. Then turn down the heat and cook on low heat for about 15 minutes.
- Add salt, hot pepper, tomato paste, sugar, finely chopped onions, and starch. If necessary, add coconut milk or water. Stir, bring to the boil, turn off the heat and stew on low heat until peas are ready.

14. Zucchini ratatouille with rice

Cook time: 45 Minutes
Servings: 4

ENERGY VALUE PER SERVING:
Calorie: 360kcal
Proteins: 4.5 grams
Total Fat: 21.3 grams
Carbohydrates: 37 grams

INGREDIENTS:
Salt to taste
1.5 kg zucchini
14 Cherry tomatoes
1 Garlic tooth
1 Onion.
4 tablespoons Olive oil
4 tablespoons Long grain rice

COOKING INSTRUCTION:

- Bring a large pot of water to the boil. Sprinkle the rice, let it boil again, then turn down the heat and boil for 15 minutes until the rice is soft. At this time, finely chopped onions and garlic. Leave the tomatoes out of the skin and crumble too. Purify the zucchini and cut it into cubes.
- Drain the rice, rinse it under cold water and let it dry in a colander.

TIP TO THE RECIPE:

Warm up the olive oil in a pan, send the onion and garlic to fry over low heat for 2 minutes, then add the tomatoes and cook for another 5 minutes.

Then send a zucchini to the same frying pan, salt it, cover it with a lid and cook, sometimes stirring, for 35 minutes. Add the rice, stir, and serve immediately.

Conclusion

Although there is no evidence that weightlifting vegans need to take creatine for maximum results, taking creatine seems safe in the quantities studied, and can probably improve performance. Sports additives companies claim that creatine synthesized without the use of animal products.

Carnitine

Carnitine (also known as L-carnitine and Acetyl-L-carnitine) is an amino acid that forms in the liver and kidneys. It is also found in meat and dairy products, but very little in plant foods. Carnitine is essential for burning most fats. Therefore, carnitine supplements are advertised by food additive companies as a means of weight reduction. However, the reality is that most people (non-vegetarians) who have taken this supplement have not lost weight. The impact of carnitine intake on weightlifters and bodybuilders has not been studied.

People whose diets contain less fat and more carbohydrates tend to have lower levels of carnitine. When carnitine intake is low, less carnitine is excreted.

Vegans and Lacto - vegetarians, have lower levels of carnitine in their blood. In one study, scientists believed that a lower level of carnitine in vegetarians is not an unhealthy indicator. It is not known whether a lower level of carnitine affects sports results.

Non-vegetarians usually get 100-300 mg of carnitine a day with food. For this reason, a vegan intake of 100-300 mg/day seems safe if they decide to take the supplement. In one study, 120 mg/day supplementation for two months did not increase plasma carnitine levels in 11 vegans, while urinary carnitine excretion increased. This means that most of the carnitine was excreted with urine, although there is a possibility that some of the carnitine was used for the body's needs.

There are side effects of taking large doses of carnitine. In one study, taking 2000 mg of carnitine twice a day caused nausea and diarrhea in 5 out of 18 people.26

Note that Solgar produces carnitine by yeast fermentation of beet sugar.

Before the competition.

Bodybuilders use a wide range of methods, some of them quite extreme, to get rid of fat and increase muscle size in weeks and sometimes even days before the competition. This book contains recommendations for increasing muscle mass and reducing fat deposits as much as possible, in the hope of reducing the desire to get involved in extreme pre-competitive strategies.

Made in the USA
Middletown, DE
20 February 2020